Liberty City

By Travis Williams

LIBERTY CITY

This book is designed to provide information that the author believes to be accurate on the subject matter it covers and is written from the author's personal experience. In the text that follows, many people's and company's names and identifying characteristics have been changed, so that any resemblance to actual persons living or dead, events, companies or locales is entirely coincidental.

Any references to resources and materials produced by other entities are purely the author's own interpretation. The author does not imply an endorsement from any of the sources cited within this book. The photos in this book were taken in Miami, Florida by Laronda Black

Liberty City

Copyright © 2022 Travis Williams
All rights reserved. Neither this book, nor any part of this book, either print or electronic, may be used or reproduced in any form or by any means without the express permission of the author, except for the use of brief quotations in a book review. Failure to comply with these terms may expose you to legal action and damages, including copyright infringement.

ISBN: 978-1-959667-04-9

Published by Pa-Pro-Vi Publishing
www.paprovipublishing.com

Printed in the United States of America

LIBERTY CITY

DEDICATION

I dedicate this book to all of my grandchildren in hopes they will understand my upbringing and find balance in their lives. I do not want them to get caught up in the peer pressures of the world and the glitz and glamour that Liberty City has to offer.

To my readers, friends, and family; this book is a testimony of my life experiences while growing up on the streets of Dodge City, now known as the notorious Liberty City.

Visitors, I hope this book gives you a glimpse into Liberty City and sparks a desire for you to want to visit us.

For those of you who are in the streets of Liberty City every day trying to break those generational curses, this book is for you.

LIBERTY CITY

This book goes to all the hustlers, hoodlums, players, co-artists, pimps, drug dealers, gamblers, goons, rappers, gangsters, and the entire Liberty City community.

This book is dedicated to the people who survived the Liberty City environment that swallowed up so many from their unconscious struggles of survival by death or jail.

To the people of Liberty City incarcerated in the prison system, as time passes, you will find that you wasted your entire life away for people who would not sacrifice their freedom for you. They abandon you before you even make it to trial and leave you alone to think and face the reality of doing this jail time by yourself.

If you don't have a support system, a devoted wife, girlfriend, or family member that would stick by your side while in jail to assist you mentally and financially, it makes the time even harder.

Make sure you don't entrap yourself in an environment of servitude for people who can't handle the struggle with you.

LIBERTY CITY

We're all divided in the oceans of illusions, I'm trying to swim from something bigger than me.

I
INTRODUCTION

I grew up in Liberty City, when my mom and dad moved from Overtown. I attended Holmes Elementary, and Edison Park Elementary, then I transferred to Little River Elementary, because my dad's income changed. That's where most black people lived during those times. My dad was employed at the Seaboard Railroad where he earned enough money to move his family into a middle-class neighborhood.

Our area was segregated where the black people lived on one side of the wall and the white people lived on the other side. The wall divided the houses. On the other side of the street was the Pork & Bean Projects. In the front of our house was an apartment complex named the Knight Manor but we called it the Village. I attended Allapattah Middle School, and Robert E. Lee Middle School. My sophomore year, I started school at Miami Northwestern Senior High. I played basketball my first year and was voted Most Improved Player. Later in my senior year, I won second team

All-City, that's now called All Dade Team. After graduation, I attended Miami Dade Community College (New World Center), now known as (Wolf-son Campus).

Due to the changes in my environment I didn't go off to college because I wanted to stay home to help my mom. My dream was to relocate my parents to another neighborhood. My goal was to be an entrepreneur to provide for my family, however, my life took off in a different direction that lead to me serving 30 years in Federal Prison. I was the 1st person that Atlanta, Georgia tried to prosecute under the death Penalty charges for the Rico Law (Racketeer Influenced and Corrupt Organization).

CHAPTER ONE
DODGE CITY

When people talk about Miami, everyone talks about the other side of the bridge where they have numerous luxury mansions. Fisher Island is one of those places and the only way to enter that community is by boat Ferrier. Star Island is where famous people such as actors, basketball players, bankers, entrepreneurs, and millionaires have their homes.

Across the bridge is where the exotic nightclub life exists. The world-famous Fontainebleau Hotel is located along the stretch of Collins Ave, where the beach lines the coast for several miles. Several different restaurants, apartments, and novelty shops located on Lincoln Road, Washington Street, and other Avenues also host events on Memorial Day and other holiday weekends.

They have visitors from all over the world that would come to see shows at the Filmore Jackie Gleason Theatre.

LIBERTY CITY

West over the bridge from Miami Beach is a different type of atmosphere or a neighborhood that experiences drive-by shootings, drugs, and frustrated residents who lack healthcare and jobs in the community. Liberty City elected County Commissioners who promised change while running for office. Some delivered, while some did not. I grew up in the streets of Liberty City, highly known for the television show, The First 48 and the world-famous 15th Ave.

Miracles Restaurant, Mr. Wonderful Store, Hollywood Swingers, and many other corner stores lined the streets. Numerous trap spots lined the Ave. throughout the alley, and there is a location on every other corner set up in the hood. There is a Housing Project in Liberty City also known as The Pork & Bean Projects. So much has changed in this neighborhood. The jungle still exists, but the leaders found another way to show bias and not be so direct with many situations.

The culture has changed and evolved with White Americans, Cubans, Haitians, and Blacks living among one another in the Liberty City housing projects and throughout the neighborhood. I grew up in the 1960s when a wall divided the projects and the area of the single-family home where I was raised. My family was the first African American family on the block of Northwest 67th Street and 10th Avenue. This was before the White Americans started moving out when the African Americans migrated into the neighborhoods. I grew up in Liberty City, where many black families came from the City of Overtown. They moved to Liberty City to give their children and themselves a better life that involved education and summer jobs. The trend we experienced from Overtown grew abroad in the city, and the past became the future of the city. I was molded by my environment. I lived in a community that was considered a middle-class area.

LIBERTY CITY

CHAPTER TWO
AROUND THE WAY

Our homes were between two major complexes, The Pork & Beans projects, and The Village. You either had to fight or fold to live in this community. I grew up as a quiet child who had dreams of taking my mom and dad out of the middle-class area that in reality, was the Hood. Although I didn't live in the projects, I would frequently visit these places because this was where my classmates and friends lived. In my younger days, I wasn't looked upon as a hustler or a thinker, but as time progressed, I gained a reputation that was known to have a level of non-tolerance for foolishness.

When you're looked upon by your peers this way, nobody wants to deal with people who have a strong reputation. People in the city seem to only understand violence and money. Many don't respect people or money because they don't understand the value of friendship, the value of the dollar, or the purpose of obtaining money. There are millions of dollars flowing through the streets of Liberty City.

Liberty City is home to some world-famous people. It is home to some of the best Pimps that worked and hustled on the streets of Liberty City. These are the places where people went to see or "obtain" a working girl, a Madame, or Prostitutes from the world-famous Biscayne Blvd., and anywhere along Northwest 79th street, the Pool Hall B. K. A. The Palace was where many women used what they had to get what they wanted and to make money for their Pimps. The Player's Ball was held practically every Year on Biscayne Blvd & 79th street inside of the Biscayne shopping plaza, to see who would win the Pimp of the year Contest.

Biscayne Blvd was the home to one of the hottest clubs in the Miami. Big Daddy's 8600 club location had a huge clientele that frequented that club on weekend. You will find anyone who had a name for themselves partying here. All of the hustlers, gamblers, drug dealers, pimps, and women hung out at this establishment especially, on Sunday night you could see the crowd of people hanging out in the parking lot. Crap games were held behind any parked cars in the lot, you could hear the customers before you could see them entering the parking lot due to the loud music playing from their cars.

LIBERTY CITY

People kept personal ice chests & liquor in liter bottles, & six packs of beer in the trunk of their cars because the parking lot would have just as much action going on outside as the inside of the club.

CHAPTER THREE
THE HOOD

However, outside of 15th Ave another well-known hustling spot where the boosters and drug dealers set up traps was the 1240 building. The front side was called 59th street and the back of the building was 58th terrace and 12th Ave. This historic hustling spot is where many people started and built their names and reputation to become the drug icons of Liberty City. They became known all over the world and all eyes were on them. We can't forget the most vicious street of them all, 61st Street. From 13th Ave to Northwest 17th Ave, 61st Street is where the Soul Survive DJs lived. They played most of the music at the High School dances.

On 61st street is where you could buy pills, alcohol, a shot of liquor, and purchase clothes from the booster, frozen cups, and chicken and fries, as well as go to Curly store on the corner of 14th Ave & 61st Street.

LIBERTY CITY

One of African Square Park entrances was on 61st & 14th Ave. The community residents sat at different tables to play checkers, and the man who owned Miracles fried conch fritters in the back of his car, the world-famous Conch Key Wonky sold us Dress Conch and boiled eggs. The elephant and Gemini trap spots were between 15th Ave and 17th Ave on 60th Street and 61st Street.

Around the corner on 60th street between 13th and 17th Ave, you had the dollar marijuana joints, the insured trap hole, and the two famous pimps living in the community with their families. The children huddled at Mr. Harry's corner store every morning before school for those goodies to sneak into their classroom. Liberty City has numerous spots that were the highlights of the day at any moment of the day. Liberty City is home to several communities.

The Village apartments better known as Knight Manor Apartments are just a block from the Miami Northwestern Senior High School, known as The Mighty Bulls. This is where many known hustlers derived from. We can't forget about the Graveyard, Scott Projects, and the Larchmont Projects. The Ghetto Style DJs used to play music at African Square Park and Rock Creek Park on Saturday, Sunday, or any Major Holiday. People came from as far as Overtown and the Barhay to come dance in these parks. There were a lot of different cars driven by the hustlers and the drug dealers. They drove everything from Cadillacs, Convertibles with trus and vouges, to hang out alongside the streets next to the parks to show off their vehicles.

CHAPTER FOUR
THE PROJECT

There are several other housing projects in Liberty City. You have Edison Projects, across the street from Edison Senior High and around the corner from Edison Park Elementary School. The New housing projects are on Northwest 19th Avenue and 73rd Street, across from the Scott - Carver Homes projects. Victory Homes Housing Projects on Northwest 75th Street and 7th Avenue across from Jumbos Restaurant. Olinda Housing Projects is across the street from Olinda Elementary School. P.S.U.

Housing Project (Project State University) is across the field from Charles R. Drew Elementary and Middle School. Several people from these communities frequent the Tacolcy Center for after-school activities or basketball, cheer, & football. Scott & New homes went to Poinciana Park for cheer and football. The community would gather and watch the children play optimist football and basketball games.

This was always fun because the winners had bragging rights.

Once the Christmas break arrived, everyone would be waiting on Christmas Day to meet up at Manor Park. We would skate on the outside skating ring in the park and ride our bicycles. We would have on our dickie screwdriver jeans with bandanas tied on the side pocket of our jeans or around the collar of our neck. We wore our canvass (Chucks) or deck shoes with our plaid shirts. The Space funk D.J.s were on the ones and twos at Manor Park on Christmas Day.

Back then, everyone treated each other like family. We looked out for each other. We put our resources together to help wherever needed. With all the drugs being sold and fights breaking out, there was always a need in the community. There was a sense of pride and respect for the women and children in the community. They were off limits to anything that was happening between an individual that was hustling in the streets.

Due to our misguided loyalty in the African American community of supporting Black-owned businesses throughout the city, other nationalities have moved into our communities and monopolized as being the number one consumer of purchasing non-tangible items such as hair, clothes, shoes, and nails. There is a lack of support for the

Black owned businesses as it relates to loans and funding to rebuild enterprises affected by the environment and declining property value. Liberty City has always been the hub for legal and illegal activities. We still have some Black-owned businesses that still stand in our community.

CHAPTER FIVE
TASTEBUDS

In the community, Brewster's store on 15th Ave. & Northwest 70th Street and Miracles restaurant sells some of the best Conch Fritters, Fish sandwiches & burgers. On 71st Street & 15th Ave. Davis, Sc hoolies, Moms, Esther, and Jumbos were some of the best Soul Food Restaurants in the City. Liberty City was full of activities. Back in the day, we had teen disco places where the teens could come together to have a good time. Pac-Jam game rooms had pinball machines, pool tables, and jukeboxes that played music that we would turn the floor into the soul train line. We would have dancing contests on the spot while we ordered chicken & fries, hot dogs, burgers, and soda pop to enjoy with friends while chilling. Jumbo's restaurant, which was reopened, was where many famous people came to eat while visiting Miami.

It was the after-hours spot for teenagers when they left the skating ring or the high school dance. Burger King on 54th Street and 7th Ave. is where everybody went after the

West had a football game. The parking lot used to be on swole, while music blared from cars. To this day, Liberty City still holds a level of excitement. Somewhere down the line, the street code changed, and our communities have never been the same. Nowadays, parents are burying their young children at an alarming rate due to the gun violence in the neighborhoods. Murders and shootings go unsolved because of the streets' code of silence or the lack of evidence provided to the Police. Miscommunication and lack of trust in the Police are why the streets handle "business" in their own way.

    A lot of stuff goes on in the hood that involves the Police and certain individuals and their families. So, they won't ever confide in the law enforcement officers unless they're paid, confidential informants. Yes, we have confidential informants in the Liberty City area. Many unsolved cases could be solved if they invested the resources into the community concerning innocent children in the streets of Liberty City. The motto, no women, no children, was the code for the hood families. When settling a beef in the streets, women and children were totally off-limits. Children are our future to breaking generational curses and carrying on our legacy for the family to exceed the next level.

CHAPTER SIX
ANY GIVEN DAY

In today's society, the youth have a different mindset about the streets. In my day, we never took on someone else's culture. Miami has always been known for setting trends, like stacking the mouth full of golds (placing golds at the top and bottom of your mouth), and sporting the Cuban links necklace and bracelet, along with the rope chain and the huge chunky jewelry.

Certain gang members, and just about everyone who was of age in the neighborhood, would frequent the indoor skating rink known as the Superstar Rollerteque, located on the corner of Northwest 79th Street and Miami Avenue,. Liberty City is well known for having some of the greatest high school athletes from highly respected schools: Miami Northwestern Senior High (Bulls), Miami Central Senior High (Rockets), Miami Edison Senior High (Red Raiders), and Miami Jackson Senior High (Generals). Many college scouts come to recruit star players from these high schools for their college programs. Whenever Miami Northwestern or Miami Edison didn't have a dance in their school gym, we all went to African Square Park to dance. That would be the spot to hang for the weekend. The ghetto style DJs would set up and bring the noise and the block would gather to party. Some of our well-known rappers are from Liberty City. Some of the unconscious found themselves within the walls of prison and became some of the best authors, artists, boxers, and fashion designers in the country.

Liberty City is the home to some of the first known gangs such as the Manor Park Rangers, the 22nd Avenue Players, and the reputed Miami Boyz, who were known for taking the drug game into other cities all over the United States. Their reputation is derived from what's going on in the city. *The First 48* highlights murders and other crimes committed in a particular community. This TV show established Liberty City as one of the most violent neighborhoods in the world. I don't knock anyone else's movements. But it wasn't us, we always rep the bottom.

Whenever I tell someone I'm from Miami, the first thing they say is, "Oh, you all have beautiful beaches. I know you enjoy the beaches. Oh, and how far are you from the Pork n Beans Projects?

LIBERTY CITY

Is it really dangerous over there?" What people from other cities don't realize is that Miami natives work most of the time and don't really go to the beach unless it's a holiday. And yes, it's dangerous anywhere in Liberty City, not just in the Pork n Beans.

LIBERTY CITY

CHAPTER SEVEN
CHOICES

The Pork & Beans (also known as Liberty Square) is the first public housing community built in the United States and is considered as one of the most deadly and dangerous. When someone dies, it's just another day in the 'hood. It's not that we're numb to the violence. It's just that that's how certain situations in Liberty City are dealt with. Too many people play with guns and are killing in vain; they're misusing guns by putting themselves in positions where "you live by the gun, you die by the gun" in the streets. They must realize that taking another individual's life doesn't serve any purpose for them. People who really like to shoot guns and are infatuated with all the gun play in the streets should join the army where they can receive training, benefits for themselves and their families, and not end up in jail for killing someone because they will only discharge their firearms in combat.

The 'hood code says you should stand ten toes down in your community; go hard for your 'hood and rep where you are from. But as soon as trouble arises, people vanish from your surroundings and leave you for dead. Don't sacrifice your worth to find out later in life that what you sacrificed for was an illusion and, your sacrifice was all in vain. Next thing you know, you're missing out on raising your children, and you've spent many years behind bars transitioning from a young healthy man to an older man. As the years go by, you can't do anything but sit back and watch yourself grow old in a 6 x 9-foot cell because of the choices that you've made. As your time in prison passes by, you soon realize that you faced so many disappointments in life from the people who are supposed to love you, and you feel like you've lost so much control of your life.

Remember to never put yourself in a bind that gives someone else control over your life. Walking blindly will place you under this duress. So, when you're on your journey in the 'hood, make smart choices; never make a decision with clouded vision because in the 'hood it can only lead to the grave or prison. If you ever return home from regaining your freedom, even if you're not in the streets anymore, you still have to be ready for the streets and the new rules of the game because, those same people who left you for dead will start showing up again like nothing ever happened. Then when you make the choice not to deal with them because they showed you how they felt about the relationship you had with them, they become defensive and act like you shouldn't have your guards up. Suckers never respect the game.

CHAPTER EIGHT
RUMORS AND WARS

A bullseye is placed on your back when you make a choice to separate yourself from your previous associates due to situations or circumstances that may have caused a rift between you, or if you feel like you're ready to go to the next level. You realize that people are only loyal to you in your presence and are elated about what you can provide for them. Suckers try to phase the standup guys out, then they try to keep them in hard times by placing their foot on their necks. They don't want to see the standup guy come up in the 'hood. So, they start false rumors and gossip about how he's moving to as many people as possible who would listen to their story instead of helping the standup guy change his life.

Solid people in the 'hood are looked upon as fools because they help those in need without them asking, especially if they have any children or the other parent is deceased or incarcerated. See, in the 'hood everybody has a story, so when you know a person is in need you just provide for them to save the person the humiliation of having to ask for help. Regardless of anyone's lifestyle in Liberty City, they have pride. Dudes that folded when they went to prison will come home and the other rats will throw them a party for the 'hood to enjoy and put a little money in their pockets. But the Robin Hoods - the solid dudes from the 'hood – don't receive anything and are left to fend for themselves because the people know that eventually, they will land on their feet. As I said earlier, the mindset has changed in the streets of Liberty City. It used to be no man left behind. Now it's every man for himself.

CHAPTER NINE
WEED AND SEED

Everyone thinks they're a real nigga in a world of anarchy. That could be possible, but under the laws of consequences the burden of judgment wears on the subconscious, and the realities of life set in. Back in the day, Liberty City's atmosphere was full of hustlers. That still hasn't changed. We have a fluctuation of drugs in the city. But times have rotated just like the fashion trends. Cocaine prices have skyrocketed to where the prices were in the 60s and 70s. This method of weed and seed weeds out the players who are not supposed to be in that lane. When times are flooded, everybody and their mama tries to get in the game.

Although the prices were high, the streets were flooded with drugs that converted so many minds. Many people couldn't enter into that world, and it gave birth to a lot of bitter hearts, and those types of hearts grew hate and that hate is connected to what was broken in their souls. A few are chosen to inherit the acceptance of the mark of the beast. Many will accept the 'hood agendas, but how many will accept the signs of the test from their choices? A man can go hard in the streets and be known as a beast, an animal, a goon, a thug, a soldier, a warrior. But at the end of the day, people will consider him a fool.

Liberty City has always been a place that goes hard, and people who have adapted to outside culture and surroundings didn't have to end over zone niggas who were put down and carried into the finest. At one point Liberty City was known as Dodge City.. Even in this day and age, the people there live by "get it (or them) any way that you can," and niggas are going to do it their way. The City is going to pay you interest on what you deposit. People from the City are attention seekers and under consideration will give what is caused for. The City style is fast, the fashion is flamboyant, and the lingo is slick. The hustle is dimensional, and the hustler's style is the rainbow city. We don't stop, we *get it*. It's a lifestyle of flashiness and excitement. In our 'hood, we carry it to a different level. When you cross the line and break the code, you must be dealt with because someone's reputation is on the line.

CHAPTER TEN
THE ATMOSPHERE

When people are violated, it causes them to result to violence. The city is a flea market and a fashion show of styles where people always lurk to make something happen. It's a movie in the making. Its survival of the fittest and jungle of the have and the have not's of the hood. The people in Liberty City are known to invent all sorts of crafty ways to make ends meet. As the culture changes and different players enter the game, the titles are now placed on the youth who rep hoods outside our own. While holding down the concept of "the boys in the hood," the reality of it all, it's our hood. This isn't a motion picture, but we picture ourselves in motion to get close to each accomplishment as we search to reach different heights.

Even though gangs lurk in the streets of Liberty City, teenagers can retrieve weapons to kill a grown man. These zoned-out video mindset killers destroy the knowledge the elders share. Later on down the line, they realize that the killers on the video don't do jail time and the street game keeps going on without them as they face the consequences of their actions. Once the killer realizes he is no longer the life of the party, his life is changed forever. He will no longer serve or hang out on the street corner again.

Yes, Liberty City produces the brave, the challenger of the challengers. Those whose attitude arose from being an attention seeker grew from fear of death and discovered what their sole purpose and existence in the hood required. The city will groom you to be aware of your surroundings and follow your gut instinct to survive in the real world, no matter where you roam and call home.

During the era of the drug trade, the pimp game took a nosedive, but it's back on the rise, so the hustle continues. The drug heroin has resurfaced from the early 60s and 70s, but time has evolved into the dog food age from brown, beige, and a little white to China white mixed with a bit of fentanyl. When the trends set in, the hustlers make their moves to fit into the action. This is the hustler's mindset in Liberty. The city's atmosphere is to grind and be a stunner. This environment has groomed some of the high-profile names in the hood.

Don't get caught up in the southern language but look at the work ethic incorporated from the production. There are many soldiers in different areas of the city. I tip my hat off to the people of Overtown, A.K.A. the Towners, for moving and spreading throughout the city. Some people moved into the Brown-sub, Carol City, and the city. But although the atmosphere has changed, our youth have adopted a different style. All of us have had our turn and faded in the streets. The gang caught our children's attention because we were absent. They leaned toward the streets and the strength of their homeboys to survive. That "we got your back" type of love has been missing from their upbringing. This is the love they look to from the gangs.

CHAPTER ELEVEN
THE RIOT I EXPERIENCED

1968 was my first time experiencing a riot after Martin Luther King was assassinated. It looked like something out of a movie from the eyes of a seven-year-old child. In Liberty city, the buildings and cars were burning, and people were looting the stores. I didn't understand the wholeness of the riot at the time. All I knew was that one of our future black leaders had been killed. Cities around the world started an uprising by terrorizing businesses. They were tired of the mistreatment and lack of respect for the African American communities.

The Pork & Beans Projects was named after a guy that stood up and went hard after many cities started to riot when Dr. King was assassinated. He went to prison for participating in the riot that changed our community and the world forever. He sprang into action when another black man tried to make a dream a reality and stop the racist attacks on blacks and was gunned down like an animal.

Many would debate this, but the community honored him for his stand against injustice when he returned. To this day, the injustice remains the same among the African American communities.

Liberty City had its share of riots. The Power of our black arm is long and can stretch far if we come together. We will have more balance and control over our communities and families. Some of our communities look like fragments of pieces exploding from a bomb blown up. Due to our petty differences, we don't see the most important scope of our superpower, the country's mental wealth, to stay on top.

CHAPTER TWELVE
THE RIOT SAGA CONTINUES

To this day, the McDuffie riot was the most horrific one yet. The Arthur McDuffie Riot started on May 17, 1980. That riot started a movement of the people gathering on the wall on 62nd Street and 12th Ave. In Liberty City, 62nd Street is now known as Martin Luther King Blvd. This was where many people lined the streets to protest for a motorist that a police officer stopped during traffic. The police served him an injustice, and many people's lives were changed that day when this riot took place.

The hood felt like the police officers shouldn't have taken the law into their own hands. They relied on the mindset that gave the authorities a right to make a judgment call to use unnecessary force that resulted in someone else losing their life. The riot was fueled by the people feeling like an eye for an eye, but when they came together, they understood that the sacrifice would not be in vain. Our way of justice won't be used against us for the actions of an unbalanced authority that governs those we trust for our safety. Some people are still in jail for protesting this unfair treatment in our Liberty City community. We have some people still healing at this time due to the actions of others from this riot. Then in 1982, history repeated itself.

The thoughts were obviously not calculated. Another good African American man lost his life and was separated from his family. A community riots when there is no support or justice for the victim. Instead, the people who stand up for the injustice that happens to the victim are incarnated. The community's mindset is to make the other races feel the pain that the other families are experiencing due to the loss of a loved one from the officer's death.

When a store is looted or burned down during a riot, it's because of the unfair treatment somebody in the hood had at that establishment. If the owner is polite and respects the customers that frequent his business, they will make his store off limits and consider him straight. Since 1980, the Miami Urban community has never been the same.

Over fifty businesses were destroyed, and only ten of them chose to rebuild back into the community. There haven't been any major retailers or malls in Liberty City. These department stores didn't return to the Northside shopping Center; Sears, J'byrons, Three Sister, Learners, Pro

Feet, Kinney Shoes, Butler Shoes, Woolworth, Pantry Pride, Eckerd's, and Woolco. After the riots, they never came back to rebuild at that location.

CHAPTER THIRTEEN
THE RIOT THREE TIMES THE FIRE

The Woolworth location was transformed into a Flea Market known as USA Flea Market. Liberty Market is the Sears store's old location. This civil unrest caused over 100 million dollars in damage in Miami. Therefore, banks and major companies viewed Liberty City with a Sore Eye. To make major purchases for their homes, family, or business, the people in this community must travel far south, north, east, or west to a shopping mall.

In 1989, another Riot took place, and the community rallied again about another killing in our community. Then in 1991, another riot ensued due to another man. This started a movement in the community. The residents felt like the Police Department and the court system weren't treating them fairly. Therefore, people's emotions were running high, and feeling like there was a double standard of justice for Black people in certain parts of the community in the Miami area.

People were sick and tired of letting their guards down. They had to witness an academy professional who was not trained to stop shooting or to shoot below the waist. They were instructed to not stop shooting. The Police Department had a pattern of shooting unarmed suspects and hiding behind the badge of honor. They were killing our men for something as small as a misdemeanor. There's no justification in shooting an unarmed person and saying you feared for your life.

I believe that when people from another culture encounter African Americans, they misunderstand us. Since they're not raised in our community, they don't know our body language or lingo and the values our family instilled in us. They feel intimidated by us. They understand us better when they're raised with us in our home or community as friends or neighbors. They will diffuse any situation rather than escalate it. Because they've been exposed to that situation, they're more familiar with us as a people and understand our culture.

This is why the people who were raised outside of Liberty City and don't understand the culture shouldn't enter these arenas. They wouldn't be spooked by the activities in the hood. When accepted to the academy, they practice at a gun range to hit their target in a precise area. The people in the neighborhood are more than targets used for target practice. They are sons, brothers, fathers, nephews, uncles, or grandparents. What happened to shoot someone in the arm or legs? Why always in the spots that will kill them? Why can't they fire the weapon out of their hands and stop the person from getting to a gun but letting them live?

Many people sacrificed their freedom during the riots. They went hard for what they knew happened to the person they were protesting.

They won't be considered freedom fighters, Revolutionary, or someone who stood up for the cause. They went down in history as the forgotten and the victim, a survivor of someone coming back into a society where they have to reestablish themselves in a society where technology has changed. The job market requires more than a high school education to receive adequate pay to survive. If they can weather the storm through society after being institutionalized for many years.

CHAPTER FOURTEEN
THE FIRST 48 (THE PORK AND BEANS)

The First 48 is a criminal mini-series. The show describes us as a war zone, which places us under the eyes of those unfamiliar with many areas in Liberty City. Many go-getters were portrayed as a menace to society in the city. The Pork & Beans Projects went from standing for a cause to being betrayed as a crime-ridden neighborhood. As shots ring out, all you can hear is the sound of a mother's cry as she loses a child to gun violence.

So many people lose their lives in the Pork & Bean Project area due to cyber beef, a turf war, or gang violence. All these activities cause the body count to be high in that neighborhood. These are the same people who grew up together and did everything from slumber parties to summer camp. The hood believed it takes a village, so everybody looked out for one another.

After all of their efforts, the children still end up becoming arch enemies because their home is merely separated only by an Avenue or a Block. The beef is so strong that if you have a family member that lives in the Pork & Beans Projects and you belong to a gang, you can't visit. If they see you, there will be consequences that could end your life. The youth have become like praying mantises, actively killing each other.

Some will kill their friend, help pay for his funeral, buy the food for the repast, and tote his casket to the graveyard. Then they're captured and placed on the show to be interviewed by the First 48. They are tricked into incriminating themselves and telling why their actions caused them to commit a crime. They're portrayed as an emotional and broken soul.

Why would you say something? The law says 10, 20 to life anyway. They don't have a choice when placed in this situation because they are nervous, their hearts are racing, and they entangle themselves with their confession. The first 48 show highlights the community's negative attributes of a neighborhood being destroyed by gun violence. The show doesn't reveal that many people in that community are decent, hardworking people. The Pork & Bean project has its highs and lows, the good and the bad, just like any other urban community.

CHAPTER FIFTEEN
THE FIRST 48 (THE MYTH)

They say people in Liberty City have a reputation for entrapping themselves in certain situations and destroying the hood from an unproductive lifestyle. This type of rhetoric causes some people in Liberty City to continue adding fuel to the fire by allowing people to see they don't understand their value in the hood. But on the street, they live their life so recklessly and ruthlessly. I couldn't understand why the cast of the First 48 showed the body of the victim and the number of bullets that the shooter emptied into the body or the number of stab wounds the victim had. That when they apprehended the perpetrator, he was so remorseful.

The First 48 has exposed that the perpetrator's image is tough, but their soul is soft, and that deep down inside, they have a conscious heart just like everyone else. It shows on the first 48 that they were faking being ruthless and playing tough but have the embodiment of a cotton essence and missing characteristics of what they displayed in the hood. When crime was committed, they were broken, hurt, bewildered, seeking revenge, or coming from a place of fear. The people of the hood must understand that the biggest Flex is going hard for you and your family.

Being gangster is buying back the block to keep the families from moving out. They want to make money to put themselves in a better position, not to be bound under incarceration and be a victim of society. We must stop letting these people make us look like we're just broken and selling our souls into bondage on the streets. Liberty City's series of major crimes caused people to watch this show. The network benefited from the views and the profits. The Liberty City community doesn't benefit from anything when another Black person loses their life. When people watch this show, it's viewed as a regular tv show, but they only see the violence that has occurred.

The people are viewed as a menace to our society, not fit to live in our community, the same hood they grew up in. Even though they're somebody's son, daughter, husband, father, or wife; plus, they give us numbers that a reptile can endure. Yes, violence is being exposed throughout the city. There are consequences for those types of actions. Stop allowing peer pressure and the games played in the back of your subconscious mind cause you to lose focus on the reality of taking a life that looks like you. Some youths are misguided in today's society about what it truly means to be a homie or a friend to someone.

A study or game task force should be conducted on the inner-city youth. They take what they learn from video games into the streets of their neighborhood, taking the lives of their peers as if they are images instead of ----human beings. They need to understand the difference between games and real-life once a person is deceased. These are real people with lives and a family, not just an image or a figment of your imagination from video games. This causes a domino effect on an entire family.

One thing about the rules of the streets is the morgue holds all of us. Don't think just because you killed someone, that you can't die. You can lie on the same road you laid a body on or killed someone. Remember, we all have to die one day. So don't jeopardize your freedom for bragging rights because we all have to meet our maker one day. Don't get trapped in the legal system. The reality of your role can place you in a position for another player to profit from your consequences. Prison is a profit system. You must work and supply goods and textiles for the outside world while in prison.

CHAPTER SIXTEEN
15TH AVENUE

Many people have heard of the famous 15th Ave in Miami, Florida, located in the heart of Liberty City. It's a historical Ave from 62nd Street to 71st Street down 15th Ave. Back then, many black-owned businesses had storefronts, car washes, game rooms, clubs, and restaurants along those blocks. The most popular place along this stretch was Miracles, which served the best fish sandwiches and conch fritters. This establishment's walls had many unique designs because the owner was a professional painter and an artist.

There was Mr. Wonderful's store where all of the hustlers hung out. After school, Hollywood Swingers was where the teenagers hung out during the day and adults by night. They had disco lights and a jukebox, even though they had a DJ system, pinball machines, and pool tables. They served mouth-watering chicken or fish along with some French fries. Back in the day, 15th Ave was the hub for a meeting of the minds, all sorts of entrepreneurs, hustlers, and women would meet to make ends meet. All the players in the game on the streets of Liberty City would meet up to discuss networking and display the stylish cars they put in the game.

They would stand on the street corner showing off their jewelry, flashy clothes, and fly mouthpieces filled with either gold or diamonds while talking slick. Some of the best hustlers known by name or face hung out on 15th Ave. Plenty of women used to stroll up and down the Ave to make sure they could be seen by the men hanging out and to see what was happenings while they were on the block. Cause the girls and ladies wanted to get a glance or rap with the household names they heard ringing in the street of Liberty City.

Back then, men or hustlers were more respectful and provided for women without them asking for anything. The girls or ladies got to see who was driving what car and decided how much money a dude made by the type of car he drove. Most women would come to hang out at the car wash so they knew who drove which vehicles. The Ave was known to be a fashion show. Everybody wore the latest top-brand watches. This was truly the home of all the hustlers, robbers, thugs, goons, and even the clowns who hung out here.

You can find anybody you were looking for from the streets inside the gambling houses or just hanging out on the street corner. You could play your numbers for the dog track at the number man/woman house. Numerous music videos were shot on 15th Ave. It was the hot spot in the 70s and the 80s then things started slowing down. In the early 90s, right before 2000. To this day, the structure of 15th Ave still remains the same. Many people who made 15th Ave are either deceased, in jail, have outgrown that lifestyle, or are sitting home in front of a tv enjoying life. They know the streets don't love you as a person, but they love what you represent in the street.

CHAPTER SEVENTEEN
15TH AVE (THE HAPPENINGS)

Block parties went on practically every weekend on 15th Ave. Many Disc jockeys made their names on 15th Ave by throwing block parties at different houses and outside in front of the businesses along this stretch. People could hear the music for blocks and blocks. The music brought out people from everywhere, like Sugar-Hill, The Pork & Beans Projects, and Scott Projects from across the tracks. P. S. U. Projects, Lincoln Field, the Village, and Sugar Hill residents would gather on the curves and the sidewalk together to dance to the music. At the same time, the flashy cars were driven by the hustlers up and down 15th Ave.

Those days of fun in the sun or the nightlife in the hood allowed our community to have fond memories of growing up in Liberty City. Trust me, Liberty City has a vivid community environment where the neighbors look out for each other as the money rolls in. I can't forget the Sugar Hill Apartment Complex because it was a gold mine and a landmark of Liberty City. Most of the people there attended Miami Northwestern, Senior High School. It's like the Vegas quote. "whatever happens on 15th Ave, stays on the Ave., but that's not for this book. I'm not a whaler, but I must respect the game and the street code.

The back alleys along 15th Ave divided all storefronts from the houses and the projects. The cars were known to creep down the back alley and away from the busy strip. There was a blind area where you could coast down behind the scene to see so people couldn't spot you. It was a great place to park your car, get out, and walk around the front of the Ave. Everyone would be standing on the street corner or in front of an establishment where everybody hung out.

So many people slipped on these street corners. A lot of people had a pattern. They hung out at the same spot all the time, so people became familiar with where they would be and when they would patronize certain storefronts or game rooms. This behavior causes too many people to pay the price for their life. They were slipping or sleeping while hanging out in the hood. I'm not upset with y'all for taking care of matters in the street designed by the street code. It's part of the struggle that helps develop a man hunting skills.

CHAPTER EIGHTEEN
15TH AVENUE (THE RULES OF THE GAME)

Sometimes people can't change, and they get stuck in the game. Only fools don't elevate and keep themselves from evolving to stop their past from repeating itself right before their eyes. Change is like a needle in a haystack. You have to know when to grow and when to fold them and move on to bigger and better things to improve your life. It's hard to find it in the heart of a man. Remember, the game doesn't change, but the players of the game do. 15th Ave is historical, but due to the gentrification that brings about change in Liberty City's environment. The revitalization of man can change the sacrifice of a misguided man in vain.

Although our parents raised us in the heart of Liberty City. We should respect the struggle and not allow our parents' sacrifices to be in vain. We should benefit from the labor they provided us. They did the best they could with what they had at the time. Why should we give our lives to system that didn't benefit our mothers and fathers? For those of us who had both parents in our lives and at home, the least we could do is become productive members of society and positively contribute to this world.

Many fathers are absent from their child's lives due to them being incarcerated or deceased. However, a child doesn't understand that life goes on once the Father goes to jail at an early age. These children grew up knowing and misunderstanding that their Father didn't love them. People don't realize that a father plays a significant role in a household. So, when he's missing, the children fill most of their time with people in the streets, and they can't stand up to the peer pressure of the hood and the glamour of the streets and join a gang to make them feel like they belong to fill that void.

CHAPTER NINETEEN
15ᵀᴴ AVENUE (THE SCENARIO)

Liberty City is the Las Vegas of the hood. 15th Ave is the back porch of the highly renamed Pork & Bean Projects. Over the years, the players have changed, but the game remains the same. Some of the storefront owners have changed over the years. You can still visit Miracles to buy a good cup of conch salad or conch fritter or a fish sandwich. Most of the building structures throughout Liberty City are still the same. The Pork & Beans is currently being remodeled due to the unprecedented crime rate in the housing projects. It's business as usual in certain parts of the hood.

Many people have come and gone, and we have to grasp the concept and acknowledge the potential of Liberty City. We must understand the environment and enjoy the scenery cause we have been using the milk and syrup concept for too long. We led a life of misunderstanding and miscommunication in our hood. It's time to get rid of the syrup, live in the flow of milk and honey, and eat off the land. 15th Ave is where we grew up, and it's not a window to South Beach. We shouldn't have to be looking from the outside into 15th Ave to survive the streets of Liberty City. Therefore, this acknowledgment goes to all past and present establishments on 15th Ave that survive in those times. While living by the street codes of the city, we stuck to the script and the blueprint implemented.

The shells ring out in the highways and byways of Liberty City so we can grow up from our petty differences. We can't agree, so we all must learn to agree to disagree. You can sit on something and know that someone is wrong in a misunderstanding, which doesn't cause death. In reality, we not only kill the people from Liberty City but also destroy the business and purpose of 15th Ave and our historical black Wall Street.

CHAPTER TWENTY

LIBERTY CITY

THE WEST (MR. P.)

The High School I attended in Miami was named Miami Northwestern Senior High School. We called my alma mater West, the home of the Mighty Bulls, located in Liberty City. Northwestern is a Historic Black High School. This school has produced some of the best Doctors, Lawyers, and pro athletes with some of the best high school records in the nation. It was our "lean on me" style Principal 'Mr. John Henry Peavy 'who was our crazy Joe during my time in high school. He was an inspiration to our school.

He made an enormous impact on every student he came across that attended the West while he was the Assistant Principal. He stayed on us to get an education. He had an open-door policy, where he made himself available to talk to you about your schoolwork, your personal life, or whatever situation you were involved with. He was the Father figure that many of us needed. He stayed involved with the students outside the school by visiting homes and talking to our families. He would run us to class if he saw us hanging in the hallways.

If he saw us skipping school in the village apartment complex across the street from the school, he would come over and run us through the neighborhood, yelling, " Oh, don't run now. I know all of your names. Trust me, no matter if it was five or ten people he saw, he's calling all of your parents. If they didn't answer, he would be sitting in your living room when you got home. He even knew your clothing, when he saw you, and who you were with. Everybody knew, including your grandparents, by the time you got home from school.

You knew you were in trouble once he saw you. He was the Assistant Principal that ran the school like he was the 'Principal.' Everyone and everything went through him. He was an inspiration and an encouragement. He built our self-esteem and made us believe we could accomplish anything and be anybody we wanted. He instilled self-pride, values, and morals in all of us who came in contact with him. He made all the decisions and judgment calls that benefitted the school and the students. He would go to bat for all of the students in school, and he took time out with you to help you accomplish your goals. He kept a close eye on those who struggled through school extremely close to him so they could make it to graduation. If a student had college offers, he would help him position himself to ensure he would qualify by assisting with college applications.

When dealing with children from an inner-city school, you have to create a positive environment for the cause of the children's foundation. If you were a troublemaker, he would weed and seed the students with the poisoned mind and help them develop into successful students. He demonstrated his dedication through his work ethic. He was the sideline coach at all of the high school basketball games. He would be running down the sideline next to you while you steal the ball from the other team, saying it's 'showtime' that meant let's make these points.

At the High school football games, he would run into the end zone whenever a receiver or a running back caught a pass for a touchdown. He would run down the entire football field along the sideline. Because; of the different activities at the school, like the Pep Rallies, where we were hyped. They named 71st Street in Liberty City John Henry Peavy Jr. I have many fond memories of every week while attending school. Mr. Peavy was a stand-up man in our community, representing our culture to the fullest.

CHAPTER TWENTY-ONE
THE WEST (PRIDE)

LIBERTY CITY

Our school marching band always put on a dynamic performance, along with the majorettes, drill team, and cheer squad. Everyone would show off and keep the football players hyped. We had a powerful football team that performed on the field and made us feel like all we did was win. We couldn't wait until halftime to see that show. It was an honor to be a Bull.

The Bulls Pride was powerful. Other schools looked at the Bulls as arrogant. It was really the sense of purpose and development that was instilled in us from the school's very roots, which goes deeper than the hood. The public school is an experienced eye opener to a naive mindset of going into the world unconsciously. It prepares you for the real world. The West is my heart and soul. I'm proud to have come from Northwestern, the school of hard knocks and a learning environment.

Our school was one big family, regardless of what side of town you lived on. The staff and students supported every team that played sports at the West. Once you entered the West, we were all considered Bulls. The school held us to specific standards, even when it came to learning and friendships. Whenever our school played another team in any sport, our school would show up in massive numbers and support our fellow classmates by cheering them on because it was the West against everybody.

There are so many memories that came out of the walls of that school. You could never recapture those memories. When I looked back, I thought about some of the people who failed some classes just to repeat the same grade over and over. They wanted to attend school for other reasons and weren't ready to face the real world because they felt safe and secure while attending the West.

At Miami Northwestern Senior High, we pledged our loyalty. The walls of learning were filled with dignity. I walked the halls of knowledge that I can't forget. The guiding hand has shaped our destiny. Wherever we roam, we will call this home. Northwestern, our own Bulls pride, was an experience. It was a shaping that prepared us for going into a world. It got us ready for the challenges that were ahead of us. Be strong, think big, and grow powerful. This is the development of our minds.

CHAPTER TWENTY-TWO
THE CRIB

The Crib is a term we use to describe the City of (Miami.) Some of us use the terminology, The Bottom to identify the location. The culture represents the town. The spirit of a hyped environment would give any visitor that southern feeling, with its flashy flair, speed boats, fast cars, and music. It's the home of the dropped music inside the car that you could hear from a couple of blocks away. They have the slick talkers, the worldwide concept of, that's my homie and the Home of the Bass. In Liberty City, we had full grills in our mouths and permanent gold teeth as teenagers or once we reached adulthood.

The Home of King Street is where everyone gathered back in the days to catch a "bad" honey or show their toys off and display the achievements from their hustle. It's nothing like the Crib; we had a lot of excitement and fun. We used to take the tops off our cars and feel the sunshine on our heads while the girls let their hair blow in the wind. You must have a representative on the passenger side. The girls in the City are known for their banging bodies and holding their natural frames as cornbread fed.

LIBERTY CITY

Liberty City has any kind of fruits and vegetables you can think of. You could stop by the fruit stand on 62nd Street and pick out what you like or get it from the Flea Market already made in several different ways. At the Flea Market, you can buy green mangoes, cucumbers, and pineapples with vinegar, salt, and pepper inside the containers. Driving off the expressway through Liberty City, you could get peeled oranges, Spanish limes, or bullets. You could always tell which business was the best by the crowd or the long lines.

How could I forget about Royal Castle? After leaving the club like Big Daddy's Lounge (8600) or the 119th location and any other club, the skating ring (Superstar Rollerteque), everyone would hang out at Jumbo's for those world-Famous Shrimp and fries. The crowd would move to the parking lot and line the side of the road in their cars. Bk (Burger King on 54th Street & 7th Ave. was the biggest hangout spot in the City after the (West) high school Football games. Speaking of the Fish Markets throughout the Liberty City area, they specialize in certain food items at every location.

Bottom Dollar Fish Market was known to have the best prices, and U Buy We Fry on 17th & 75th Street allowed you to pick your own seafood from their display, and they would fry it up for you. On Fridays, the parking lot was full of people. At the 79th Street Fish Market on 8th Ave, they made a mean Conch Salad and some well-seasoned fish. The City's soul food dishes are on point, especially on the seafood tip and the soul plates. The old-school ice cream trucks used to come scrolling through the hood.

CHAPTER TWENTY-THREE
THE NEIGHBORHOOD

Everyone wants to be known in the City. Everybody knows Moore Park is where you go to get your workout on. When you're making your rounds in the hood, you must go holla at ya boys on 18th Ave and pay your respect and go under the tree on 22nd Ave and show your face to see how lucky you can be with rolling the dice. On certain days you'll see the youth riding their motorcycles, popping wheelies all through the City while stopping or blocking traffic like they have the key to the City. It's a feeling to experience as a sightseer.

You must come and live out the experiences on the other side of the bridge in the heart of Liberty City. On 79th Street and 7th Ave, we have several Gentlemen's Clubs. There are strip clubs like, Take One, King of Diamonds, The Rolex, The Office, and many others we use to entertain us. To get "fly," you must stop by Rasool's Menswear or the 79th Street Flea Market and get your gear up at a Black-owned clothing store. All sorts of things happen on the other side of the bridge. It takes a lot to survive in the hood. South Beach is one of many places that have storefronts and restaurants. We had Greene Shoes and Sons for our shoe repair. King Tailors for clothing tailor-made, Three Sisters, and Learners.

In Liberty City, we have some beautiful babes and not in the token of children. Again, as I said, they have hood bodies. Those that make you want to hit a few corners throughout the City. I know you won't be disappointed because the hood looks like Africa, filled with beautiful black sisters everywhere. They will match up with any made-up body from a cosmetic surgery center. They're gorgeous, and some of them are real head-turners. I know you are going to see something you want. You have to behave if you have a woman.

There are many different types of babes out here. They come in several sizes, colors, and fashions...but, make sure they are age appropriate due to their maturity. Our queens are loyal, intelligent, and strong; some can even throw down in the kitchen.

CHAPTER TWENTY-FOUR

LIBERTY CITY

UNSPOKEN OF AREA

Tourists come to town expecting to see the city lights and wiggle their toes in the sand of the beautiful beaches in Miami. They want to enjoy the sights, visit the places and see the different cultures. The town hurdles over the bridge, and the unknown people give a face to the Miami brand. Liberty City has been the graveyard of the unconscious mind because most people don't understand the purpose of the environment of Liberty City. There are trials and errors on our journey in each of our cities. We must channel our third eye and understand that an author designs the books we are placed in. Each area is a project, so we can't get caught up on the structure of the title.

We were born in a master project designed for us to fall by the wayside of its design. If we get caught up in the matrix of the plot, then we will fall victim to all the varieties of the snares that victimize anyone less minded. It's said nothing good comes from a program designed for us to be victims. But when you understand what happens, do you let bygone be bygones? Or do we condition ourselves to take on the challenges of our experiences in life? The conscious understand their cross. They bare it and allow it to be an experience to uproot the weeds of their lives and sow better roots toward their foundation by not allowing themselves to be trapped in the darkness of their soul and find their purpose.

I lived in Liberty City but was born in Miami Beach. I was raised in the heart of the City, where I walked the streets of reality. The inland shores were supposed to be the safety of the waters. So, why are we making it to be the depth of the red sea of our own hands? It's the blood of our sisters and brothers. Should we walk around daily with the mirror in our hands, not do our hair, brush our teeth, or wash our faces? But; to see our faces aren't the original plan of a genuine concept of we are one. We confess we are real. Do you think so? I was told the real will die one time. The things we do, don't equal the balance of growth. Do you consider being the reality of what we confess?

CHAPTER TWENTY-FIVE

UNSPOKEN AREA (OF THE CITY)

The truth will set us free. Our souls are on a quest to be free. The truth of balance will scale you out of your troublesome unbalance. Liberty City is the quality or state of being free. How do we go from living in a city with the title of being free? Allowing the smoke of a king planner to enslave our mentalities to be in servitude of each one cast in the same diagram. Big City dreams! It's a dream because, in our subconscious thoughts, we know something isn't right. The soul of a man takes on its form to unconsciously survive. Not understanding the unseen hands that control the harness of an unconscious sight and our mindset.

We need to change the name to the City because; we have lost our way of Liberty. If we free our minds from the state of just existing, then the streets we roam would be made of gold, not our own blood. You must have visual control by shaking off that Matrix from yourself on the streets of Liberty City. Don't wait until you go to prison and get caught up in the trap.

Bring back the Liberty of not being fooled because; something good can come out of the plan that's against us. We're not checkmates, but we can be checkmates of a more powerful entity that created us. They try to shape and mold us to fit into a society that doesn't have our best interest in important matters. We must shake that stigma off and understand that we are the image of creativity. We all have been sucker punched, but that doesn't make us suckers. Why not liberate your own mind? We allowed the sucker punches to continuously jab us, and we're not punching bags. We know there is a pain in a punch, but at some point, we have to stop allowing the punch to connect with our bodies because it serves no purpose.

Never allow the lights to only shine on the building of the City. Make sure it shines on you. The intelligence of Liberty City has been caught up in the rapture for too long in the trickery of someone else restraining them. I'm not a preacher or a teacher but an experienced observer. One who understands that the times aren't right. There are too many bones in the valley that are not coming together to form the image of what we used to be. Dinosaur bones are put together for us to see what they used to look like, but we can't put ourselves together. We must see what we were created in the image of. Now, we aren't bees. How can something come out of the want of being? Extract it from our subconscious thought of desire to be and be that thought of being that success of mastering what you know.

LIBERTY CITY

CHAPTER TWENTY-SIX
UNSPOKEN AREA OF (LIBERTY CITY)

Although things happen in the City here and there, some people get victimized by careless actions. The same way our elders looked at us and said these children are all over the place, it applies to children today. I was raised in the 80s, and those were some trying times. A lot of money flew through the hood, and a poor hustler could panhandle a bankroll, pay their bills, and take care of all the things they needed. Through the course of the day, you can come up with a few bands. Today, you can hear the rattle of the change in the sound of a can. The time has changed from the 70s to the 80s. People didn't talk as much. If you wanted to know who had the work or if the dealer in your hood had it, he wouldn't tell you who the resource was coming from.

The '80s changed people. They use information from the streets for gossip to feel hip and spread the news to try to fit in like they are the man. Information isn't for gossip. Back in the day, like in the seventies, if you asked a guy who got the work, he would tell you to give him the money, and he would go get it and bring it back to you, but in every era, actions change. Today, the youth get on Facebook and YouTube and turn themselves into the police by showing their hands and faces. By telling about what they did to their enemy, posting guns and money, and rapping about how they did it. They are giving up information that the hustlers survived off of. They have to know that the police are monitoring and listening to the entire time to find out who the players of each gang are.

CHAPTER TWENTY-SEVEN

NEVER JUDGE A BOOK BY IT'S COVER

In the seventies, players of the game didn't even talk on the phone because the Feds would play back their phone recordings. They would mute all the music in the background so you could hear their conversation clearly. However, the people in the hood will say he's a real G. he goes hard. He's speaking about some real stuff and dropping jewels, but in reality, he's helping them build a case on him. When you're in the streets, you can't be speeding cause you have to think about the illegal ramifications that trigger how you're moving.

People talk too much! The rats or the snitches know what's going on in their life. They give this information to the other side so they can advance their lifestyles. They are wondering why they're on the law enforcement radar. They put weak people around them who obtain information to use later to expose them. Then they get themselves in a compromising position and can't do that jail time. People spread your business to make them look like they are down with the click and roll with the crew that knows what the happenings are. He's the same one getting pressured on each program.

LIBERTY CITY

Everybody is tough until that pressure is applied. It's like what is shown on the First 48 when they put them in the interrogation room. In every episode, the people break down by telling their side of the story to ease their consciousness. This paints a different picture of someone acting tough while carrying a gun on the street. This is what everyone does once they have been apprehended.

People don't understand that if they had enough information on you to convict you of a crime, they wouldn't need your side of the story. What they do is ask you questions so you can tell on yourself. They already have the information, so why answer their questions once they pick you up. They should just arrest you and don't debrief you about the situation. Just advise you about the charges. Since you're innocent until proven guilty, they should take you to your cell if they know you committed the crime. Everyone wants to be in the presence of those in that life. However, you are also being judged by those you keep around. The book of you doesn't fit the cover cause you can bear the consequences of that street life. Now, you're titled and labeled by the stamp of your actions from the street. You must stand ten toes down in the street and never fold under pressure.

It seems like every decade, the times change. Some people watch the hustlers rise in their community, which leads them to life in jail or dead. However, once they're released, the current hustler in the hood would throw them a party or do a movie about them. There are two sets of rules for the hood. A real Old G that stands on their square is treated like a square of the 70s. Hustlers in the 70s didn't affiliate with squares. They made them stay in school, and they couldn't enter the life of the school of Hard knocks.

The times have been reversed. They embrace the dishonesty that destroys the street game and show the man/woman who stood ten toes down no love. Then we have those who stand up against the pressure when they are in those handcuffs and thrown in jail.

On the other hand, we have some of them that are stand-up dudes, but they're also grimy and mess it up for those of us who can show and prove we're all-around good people. The good have to suffer for the doubt others have shown.

CHAPTER TWENTY-EIGHT
NEVER JUDGE THE BOOK (BY IT'S COVER)

Good men gain respect and lead by example. They understand the role of friends with benefits. Certain people will never want you to show your talent because your strength will expose their weaknesses and diminish their credibility in the hood. They want you to play a role and lay low to help the weak stay on top of their shine. You automatically become their target when you stand out from a circle of weak people. Your standards are placed in the spotlight, then they attack your image. While trying to assassinate your character in the process. Therefore, the student in the weak circle must stay with the weak crew to stay in position to maintain their status quo.

In this world, we have the haves and the have-nots, strong and weak, acceptable and the outcast. We really don't know how many people are in a position that can do what they want to do. How many can choose their own Doctor, create their own medicine, and live without the fear of receiving vaccinations or medicine laced with unknown drugs from outside resources? Our history is filled with trickery presented by those in positions when the people needed help. If this is a country of Liberty, why don't we have our own water and food?

Why are so many suffering from diseases such as high blood pressure, diabetes, colon cancer, breast cancer, and prostate cancer, along with a host of other elements? The majority controls the U. S. A. Health System that decides our expectancy from our healthcare providers. At least one of our family members will be diagnosed or die from the abovementioned diseases. When people survive the conditions, there is a state of confusion for various reasons. The Doctor underestimates your survival rate due to your life expectancy. We State our opinion about the smaller picture avoiding the bigger picture of something unfair.

The book cover is an illusion. The masters of illusion are what make us accept whatever is done. It's foreseeing the cows were falling out cause they were being fed meat instead of grass. Something causes them to eat out of the scope of their regular diet, which causes several of the health problems the world is experiencing in their bodies. These diseases aren't from natural causes. Scientists study ways to weaken our bodies to control the medicine and disease administered to society. The Doctors and the nutritionist will say to eat right? How can we, when we're under the control of the people who provide the food and know what can happen to your health when eating these foods.

LIBERTY CITY

CHAPTER TWENTY-NINE
NEVER JUDGE A BOOK BY IT'S COVER
(THE MATRIX)

We're all victims because of what we were born into. We must step outside the Matrix and re-channel the balance for the masses. Understanding and studying these conditions in our neighborhood requires a certain mindset to clean up the environment. Destroy and kill are what the weak do. They create tactics to promote wrong in a position to straighten and heal. They keep their feet on the necks of the strong so they can cast an image that they are in control of. As a Liberty City native, don't judge my mindset from the past. I'm on the standup for what's right. Suppose you were a drug dealer in the hood that sold lots of drugs.

They would say you're a Kingpin because you controlled that area, so they would get you out of that hood even if you were violent or a Robin hood. They feel you have too much influence over the domain but not those that control and oversee global affairs. What are they called with all the unbalances that have affected the masses? What are their titles? If, on the local level, we are called King Pins or Drug Lords. What are their titles if the groups are in the Matrix?

Why are millions in poor health and dying? Why are so many mentally dysfunctional and taking all types of medicines but still dying? They later discover that some of those different products cause cancer, which is wrong. Unfortunately, they get punished by the conditions that cause many to lean toward substances to help them deal with the realities. The ones on the lower totem pole are blamed for those higher up the bar. Those unseen are responsible for messing up the product of what we were groomed in the image of.

CHAPTER THIRTY
THE MINDSET

Each mindset is cultivated by its environment. If our youths have easy access to drugs and guns, most of them will use both of them. They carry guns and use them to fit in with their peers to let them know that they are down in the streets, even, if they just want a gun to show off. Most of the youth will start off trying to get money because it changes their conditions at hand, but, when the money and fame is established from the success of selling drugs then the partying from their accomplishment comes in.

Socializing and getting high takes over in their lives. They enter into another world filled with other dreams and desires that distract them from their original purpose. When you're in the streets of Liberty City, the way you conduct yourself when you're in the midst of your peers, let's them know that he or she is on the rise from their hustle. Soon, afterwards the drugs takeover and what was once a tool to change the conditions turns to an addiction. A clear mind becomes cloudy and violence starts to set in the heart. Your principles and judgement become tried and your decisions become cloudy. You begin to fill the pressure from the peers that are around you, who are watching you as you rise. Their demise edge your vision to handle your business outside of the normal business hours.

The real mob is money over the bullshit. We allow the bullshit to set in and take us off our journey to succeed. The success we wanted for our family is pushed to the back burner to fulfilled our quest. We change the gain to the game to do it by any means necessary. We lose by playing the wrong and not understanding the game is to get in and get out. We end up getting caught up in the hype of the game and miss the opportunity to seize the moment to reach another level, to better our lives.

We complain to others about the stuff that's happening in our hood. We want to bring certain things into a reality that nobody will help support while you are building your empire. Soon as you get it off the ground, the smiley faces and everyone else, wants a piece of pie as soon as its created and generating money. They loved your achievements but they didn't value your grind and behind your back they played dirty. They shoot venom and dislike that you were trying to upgrade yourself and give yourself a better life, that would place your family in a different status quo in the hood. When you establish a business that's needed in your community, and it's what the people needed all along, here comes the copycats clogging up the economy.

LIBERTY CITY

CHAPTER THIRTY-ONE
THE HOOD BIBLE 666

You must build your foundation and be in position to add value to your life if that person sees the gain in you. In order to give you that balance you need to show your talent. To build is challenging, it's a difficult situation that many short cuts themselves into. The open minded understand there are other options, other than allowing your tunnel vision to be that set back in your life. We're living in the time of weakness. The masters of weakness understand the mastery of the weakness, which keeps them in control.

They control everything, including studying the weaknesses of others. The strong wonder why it's so hard for them to get in position. They don't understand who's in control. The gods of weakness play on your vulnerability. In their reality they feel like powerful kings because they place fear in other people. This type of fear comes with terms and conditions in order to be in their presence. They speak of conspiracies theories. Their actions are the bones of the valley. It's like a toothache. Your tooth is aching but you are overlooking the bad diet that is causing it. The truth will set us free so don't be puzzled by the truth. Just understand that the students of the vigor are the ones in control.

The three sixes are known as the mark of beast. Why are these three sixes attached to things that's said to be evil? That number represent every description that's associated with evil things and the mastermind of deception. Therefore; you have to decide how to receive the concept of the image. We all have a choice to make rather its we live a life that's pleasing or life filled with turmoil.

There is a myth about the color black. The dark color has been cast into people's minds and given them an image of this color through the eyes of the Liberty City society. That image was looked upon as evil. In trying to develop another concept of a new reality, a race of people were reduced and misused. From what we were told as Black people, black cats, black goats, and the sacrificing of, and a host of other black things were evil. In the business world, when you finish any quarter or the end of the year in black, that means you had a successful year. Now go figure!

CHAPTER THIRTY-TWO
THE SHOW BOATS

There are other toys to show outside of the water. You will see them being displayed in different areas in numerous style and fashion. There are all sorts of vehicles in the Miami area. These images and styles are spotted throughout the hood. Again, you don't have to go out to the beaches or the sea to see your showboats. There are brothers and sisters that flash their styles in cars. The hustlers get down in the city. They bring the noise when they bring out their cars. That upgrade just to show the world from show boating to stunting. Bougie people have been stunting and living the high life for decades, this didn't just start in Liberty City.

Many different cultures have migrated into the Liberty City area which enhanced the show boating. Different cultures bring different flavors. They show their taste along with their culture and style. King Street brought out all of the different flavors. It was the hub of the coming out and showing what you're working with when it came to looking at your car. Everyone stood out on 71st & 7th Ave as they drove their cars down the strip.

The custom paint job on the cars were off the Richter scale and so was the boat paint, flip paints, and the Airplane paints. People had their car painted in their favorite sports team colors. These paint jobs were called the bowling ball, UM colors, Miami Heat colors, the pearl white, money green, the doo-doo brown, and the fins, which represented the Miami Dolphins You name it, we went out and got it and placed it on our prized possessions. We drove our cars while sitting up high, or low to the ground. As a low rider we were stunting at all the Black Parties, we had to come thru to show off our Golds, Jewels, and cars.

Liberty City is the home of the bass inside your vehicle. The jewelry had to be on point. Some of us wore Cuban links dripping in diamonds. The ladies had on their spinning rings with the matching bangle bracelets and earrings, with their necklace and gold chains. The Dunks fellas drove what we call spaceships, because they had so much technology inside of the car. The thrill was making them more advanced than their homeboys car. A simple push of the button made it your own style. Once your homie saw what you were working with, it thrust him back to the drawing board to figure what type of features he could come up with to top your car. The competition of styles ranged from the power vision to see how you could dig deep to bring out a style, that would impress the ladies. They women would say "oh my goodness, look at his car", "it's banging or coming thru." This is what we would say when you stood out

LIBERTY CITY

from the crowd with your styles were giving them straight pressure.

CHAPTER THIRTY-THREE
VALUES (LIFE LESSON)

In Liberty City back in the day, we had values and morals for the hood. We governed our streets and we didn't disrespect our elders. Our elders gave us wisdom and enlightened us on whatever topic was necessary for us to learn and grow. They checked us when we were wrong. In our hood, everyone was your Mom and Dad. We didn't feel violated and our spirits were lifted because they made us feel like they cared.

We helped the older people in our community, we had chores around our house, by taking care of our home it taught us family values, we cut the grass for our homes and the neighbor as well, we made our beds before leaving home to go outside anywhere. We picked up our clothes off the floor, we hung our clothes on the clothesline in our backyard once they were finish in the washing machine to help out. When an ingredient was missing we went to the store for our mom or dad while the meal was being prepared. We took the garbage out once we finish eating dinner at night and placed it out front for the garbage man to pick it up from the house on the day it was designated.

We didn't have to wait until we were in jail or prison to find a bible and ask God for forgiveness and repent of our sins. When we went on a caper and one of us was apprehended by the law, and the other person escape we didn't sing like a parrot on the other person who was with us. Back in the day, your homie or the men and women had your back, they didn't leave you for dead and if they did, we didn't parrot him out but we handled our personal business with him.

The times have changed, people have a child support mentality. They will crucified you then put the law on you. It's no justification for gossiping about people. Things can go wrong and it shouldn't be a surprise to anyone who's in the street of Liberty City. Stop feeling disappointed in the moves suckers make due to their shortcomings. If you doubt the suckers you make a play with, have a backup plan.

Do your homework on anybody you come in contact with. Go to night school on that person. If you have to question his loyalty, then that connection isn't the right face value for you. They are a more rest in peace type of person. Rest in peace if the play don't go right, we never shoot the hood up. We knew who held the bank and we had to make a deposit in it, nothing was a petty decision. There were no problems that were too big that couldn't be resolved by having a simple conversation with that person. We respected each other's opinions or feelings and found a way to come to grips with a peaceful resolution.

CHAPTER THIRTY-FOUR
VALUES (MORALS)

In the streets we held each other down, we built trust among each other. We weren't one without the other. Nothing came between us. We believed in teamwork makes the dream work and we lifted one another up. We valued each other's friendship. We didn't talk behind each other's back with secret counseling. Backbiting is a spirit, we were innocent because we knew that our sons walked with the principles of men. Nowadays, people be rocking and riding with the wind, we got to get our innocence back. Let us return Pride back into Liberty City, it's the heart of excitement and the root of the entire Liberty City.

It's the circulation to the whole city of Dade County. There are real people in every hub of the City. This book is to bring awareness to the hood of the Liberty City that I grew up in. It's not a reflection of trying to downplay any other area in Miami Dade County, it just me uplifting the Liberty City community. This book is about Liberty City and I hope that I can inspire the people to bring pride and values back to our community and inspire others to share their side of town.

The values must be restored in each neighborhood, that gives us an opportunity to become better people. We shouldn't fear the progress that we don't understand because of the nature of the environment. Our values have changed! We are not conscious and don't care about the people and the neighborhood anymore. We have started to lose our values by embracing the rats and throwing them parties when they get released from being incarcerated. A rat is like a Zombie, he has been bitten. Although, he looks like our boys, he has turned into someone else in order to survive from the choices he made by being in the streets.

The rats are supposed to lookout for their rodent brothers. When they turn, we have to check them out. He needs to be investigated and you need to stop embracing what he used to be. All stand-up dudes aren't good dudes either, because they are grimy. They make it bad for the sacrifice you made to endure. By placing fear in other people and not giving them a chance to see your worth, when you know you stood up straight, and wasn't a creep. You played fair and they crossed the line then they make you out be the villain and they're the victim. It makes you question yourself. Did I really know these guys, because they really don't know you. They have their ears to the politics of the gossip, they view you in the light of what they heard about you and not wanting to come into contact with you.

LIBERTY CITY

Get to know them for yourself because they are misguided, from the word of mouth of someone who has done you wrong. Remember, rats are always going to share cheese, it's in their nature. They are going to stick together. So, charge it to the game…it's their loss. The harsh reality is life goes on with you or without. They embrace the culture, because they have the same lingo and swag but he was turned and bitten. He's a Zombie and not Tom, John, Dick, Harry, or Joe.

CHAPTER THIRTY-FIVE
NUMB

When you grow up in an environment that many are told is a war zone, those that don't live there consider it unfit to raise a family. No matter what area in Liberty City you live in, it's the mindset of the people in the community that matters. Anyone can live in a particular area and still become a product of their environment, get caught up in the streets and be incarcerated. It's not where you live it's how you live. There are plenty of people that have graduated from high school in the Liberty City community and gone off to college. Some joined the military, some became professional athletes and entrepreneurs.

It's the mindset of being all you can be to survive in this neighborhood. We grew up in a system of living from day to day. We adjusted to that type of lifestyle because our parents were pushing us to be productive members of society. You had to be careful not to succumb to the pressures of living in a society of have nots. You shouldn't put your mind in a laboratory experiment like rats. Some people are broken from past traumas, hurt, and neglect. This stems from abandonment issues due to what they endured from someone on their journey. In life, it is hard to understand how the system in the world operates.

They must realize you can easily become a product of your environment due to the entrapments that surround your community. You have to choose which entanglements you become involved in. We have been placed in an environment to study the reaction of how men handle certain situations once problems arise. They test men like rats by breaking the mind down to see their nature so they can create a stigma towards us. There are very few people who don't turn into the laboratory experiment because they stand ten toes down and don't worry about how society portrays us as a people.

While many of us turn from humans to the nature of a rodent, many try to escape the numbness by using drugs or drinking, sometimes both to mask the reality. After the effects of the substances wear off, that same situation still exist and they fall back into that sensation again. By using other numbing skills to relieve the pain, they endure in the midst of Liberty City. Being numb teaches you how to adjust yourself around people in that environment so they will view you as normal. There are so many things that people experience while living in Liberty City that they don't have the answers for. They really don't understand the conditions they live in. At one point, there were some schools in Liberty City didn't have textbooks.

Students didn't have books to use at school, nor less to take home and complete assignments. This should never happen in today's society with all the funding and resources available. We must try to understand what makes a person become so comfortable living a lifestyle they don't see anything wrong with. The seed is planted at home. If it's checked at home, it won't walk out the door into society. It must be uprooted in order for that person to succeed in this world. When communities get weeded and seeded out, they have to rally together to keep that neighborhood intact and obtain the resources for their families to survive in Liberty City.

When things change, the people and environment changes also, because of what was instilled in them or what they learned from the streets or in their home. If we don't clean our houses, then we will be comfortable with the living conditions. If we build a system to get up each morning and shower and brush our teeth, comb our hair, and take out the garbage, then we enter into a society with an agenda of progress and not of digress. This is when we begin changing the laboratory project of grooming the mindset of an animal.

People jump and run from something as small as a rat and this how they look at the experiment. You have become numb, as if this is the way of life. if you want to be wild and can't see yourself better than a rodent experiment. Civilized people don't become numb, they understand something is wrong and come up with a strategy to overcome that situation. Something is going on greater than what they can understand in Liberty City. Just take a step back, sometimes it takes stepping out of the picture to get a clearer view of what's going on. Then we can make the necessary adjustments.

CHAPTER THIRTY-SIX
THE AFTERMATH

These images mold and shape Liberty City, It's still man that didn't come to mind. Charge it too my mind and not my heart and love for the people from my hood. Never think your images weren't important in the quest of what made this City and helped place it on the map. My quest is to reach out to those, I remember and for those I forgot or overlooked through my thought pattern, forgive me. If I missed you remember it was not intentional.

Through these images, it's our duty to reach back. I'm speaking to those who are still living. We got victimized in a war that we got trapped in while thinking it was a net to rise us out of a condition we struggle through for many years. To our unveil, it was fully planned out in our communities. They didn't care how much money we made. I learned at any time they could seize everything we had, Plus place us under their wages, killing many birds with one plan. Spreading the drugs throughout our hood and placing our people in bad health and ruining our neighborhoods. It contributed to destroying our sisters, messing up their wombs, allowing their children to be born with drug addictions and birth defects from the different types of drugs they had consumed while pregnant that caused damage to the fetus before it was born into this world. They placed us in prisons throughout the states, that caused separation from our children.

Taking away the guidance we could have provided to our offspring's. The family unit is destroyed due to lack of communication. Financial hardships are on them, not allowing them to visit the individuals incarnated. It becomes out of sight out of mind if there's not a real connection with the individuals involved and placing other elements into play. There's a system in place for the community to capture their imagination to keep the domino effect of placing us under controlled environments to enforce the rules of the prison system.

They are trapping the attention of the youth by turning themselves into a different kind of slavery. They're doing it on the pretense of being down with or being part of a gang. The City of Miami always had its own culture. We never adapted to no one else's culture. I'm not knocking anyone's groove, they have to do them and lived how they've been groomed but, even in those titles it's a plan...but that's another story. Once they are locked up, they see what and who is really real. Liberty City youths have been torn from the core of realities of the known images that has been placed in prison which has left our youths to lose respect of the direction of the cause to senseless actions.

The goal was to always get your money, move your family out of the hood and place your family and yourself in a better situation. It never was meant to destroy the neighborhood but, in the hood there are always casualties along the way. That's simply part of the game if people don't think it's right. Those who mold and shape the City has to be the Fathers of their creations. They have to stop just paying child support and sitting back and not taking on their role as a parent to lead and guide them. You have to let the youth know they don't have to go into the streets and go into battle.

The same way you attract them to create what displeases you can rise up and teach them something positive. Teach them the ropes of staying out of the way and making great decisions that will allow them to eat from a table of prosperity through freedom and safety. It's a greater movement that can be better than losing them for years to system that will break them down and benefit from them while working in prison. The hardworking Mom that did all she could to provide for them can see her child live a better life, rather than getting gunned down or placed into modern day slavery. The youth have a heart but due to situations and circumstances their hearts have turned into hate and they live hardcore towards each other.

They are in the same shape we are all in. It's easy to kill, but it's hard to be real. Every tongue confesses their realness until they are behind those bars, then the paperwork comes out showing he folded under pressure. A man dies one time, a coward dies a thousand times. He can't face his wrongs and niggas confess on the killers, then be admitted into the mental ward. On the street they say oh I'm a Killer, then make it to jail and tell on everyone they know cause they don't want to do the time. One you snitch on someone else that alters your character and who you are as a person. Everyone knows the streets comes with consequences. People enjoy the glory part of the streets.

The money, the women, the cars, the expensive restaurants and all the other lavish items that goes along with the lifestyle. When the heat comes down they fold and point the finger at the other person instead of taking responsibility for the role they played along the way. Remember, you made a choice to hit the streets no once asked or forced you to live that lifestyle while you enjoying the benefits. They say killers can't sleep at night, in prison or jail you should see how most of them cry. It sounds like a daycare center. Don't do the killing if you can't do the time. I know it's not hard to kill one of your own in your hood, but behind those doors a person turns into a fuck nigga but play in front of people and be fronting for the image and likes.

LIBERTY CITY

Suckers, get into your lane and stop lighting the fire and making the culture look bad. We have to stop letting the youth think that killing your peers makes you tough because once you're gone they won't even remember his name anymore.

CHAPTER THIRTY-SEVEN
LIBERTY CITY STAND-UP

Our people don't support each other and they hate to see others get ahead, they should be charged with a hate crime. A sucker will never like a real nigga. The sourness that they have in their hearts for a real G won't allow them to find balance in their soul. To form a union between men we have to stand up in our hood. These are our little brothers, nephews, and children out here in these streets. They're displaying and demonstrating these hate crimes on each other because that's what they see in our hood among the people they're surrounded by.

These are our children who we have lost focus on and have allowed them to take control over their mindset. In this day and age these children have the mindset that the world operates like the video games that they play and you can see those results in their lifestyles. Some of the people these children encountered are their long-lost cousin or a family member that we lost contact with. They don't know who they are pulling a gun out on, many of them only live a few blocks away from each other. These are our friends that we grew up with and our parents had us sleeping in the same bed with as children. We ate at the same table, played on the same playground. Once they became a certain age those children became their enemies because they moved out the neighborhood to another community then all of sudden they became strangers to us. The adults moved away to Overtown, Carol City, and the deep-down South.

They had children that grew up in different environments to later return to the same streets their parents grew up in. They die due to the people thinking he's from another hood. The parents have to come to grips with the fact that one of their classmate or previous neighbors killed their child. We must put a stop to these video gangsters. When the game is over, and reality kicks in, they have to deal with the real-life consequences. They won't be seeing their family or the streets again for a very long time. We're the only culture that despise or hate one another to the point we will take a man or a woman's life because of what they have, what they drive, or where they live.

Our culture has to stop displaying this type of ignorance and showing weakness in times of adversity. They need to exemplify that we're trendsetters and Kings and Queens in our dominion. Instead, we go out of our way to impress the outsiders that don't care if we live or die. Some people in this environment are stuck in a time warp that has been updated to slave mentalities and its recking havoc on our community. There's an old saying that states "they're living to impress people they don't like" by driving certain cars, dressing a certain way, wearing designer clothes and shoes, and living in a certain size house while barely getting by.

Trying to keep up with Joneses, while their children are falling by the wayside and the video games and social media are raising their children. We must bring back values and morals to our community and put back a sense of pride in our streets. Why do people go against the grain with black-owned businesses? They don't support them in our community. Our people will frequent other establishments that's not our race and pay full price but will enter a Black business and request a discount. They don't ask the other businesses for the same discount and those businesses don't invest into our communities. They direct their resources and money to the culture and country they left behind to come to America to make a better life for themselves and their families.

How did our culture allow our offspring to fall victim to a society that doesn't represent what we stand for. We've lost a grip on some of our youth due to the lack of guidance and resources in our community. Sometimes we're unaware of their lifestyles and activities until someone in the neighborhood speaks up about their involvement in the streets, or the system contacts you about them being arrested. By that time it's too late cause they're being led by people who they think have their best interest at heart by championing them and encouraging them while they're in destructive mode. This only leads an individual into a system that benefits from their ignorance. The non-supporters make the mistake of being misled and place themselves in a sucker position.

Brothers, our qualities are much greater than selling our labor to the system of an unseen hand. We say we love our Mother's, so, why do we disrespect the quality of her, and give our abilities to someone else and leave our mom with broken hearts. After all of her hard work of instilling values and morals into becoming a productive member of society. We still turn around and put our time into the streets that leads to us going to prison while trying to fit into the peer pressure of others. Once we're incarcerated we can't find at least five people to reach back and send us some money that we sacrifice our freedom for. Now, the same woman that we abandoned to live in the streets for, we now have to place a burden on her to provide money for us while we're in jail. Life goes on with you or without you. You place burdens on your mom for money to call niggas that says you're a rider or a soldier, but they won't support your living standards while in jail.

Liberty City wake up, stand up, let's be the tour to all the other parts of the city. Man we are the city, so stop laying back like (OBS). We might be physically older, but we must be wise mentally. We can't continue to sit back and allow our youth to become entrapped in a system that's being orchestrated just for them. The system has a plan for us but we must come with a plan of our own to save our youth from this system because we're the best planners. Don't wait until a funeral happens in order for us to come together. We need to support the living. It's like you're coming to support the dead. They come to your funeral because sometimes the attention wasn't there when you were alive.

THE CONCLUSION

The entire Liberty City area has changed, by demographics and ethnicity. It's the same token in every inner-city in the United States of America, We witness the same cause and effect in all of our neighborhoods. In every city there is crime. When most of these crimes take place there is a reason why and a cause and effect that applies to the rules of the game. When you are in the streets it comes with the territory these types of situations occur and you have to deal with certain outcomes such as, rivalry among peers, drugs, gambling, making, or losing money, domestic situation that involve men and women, someone intoxicated from drinking or on drugs and can become violent and you may have to defend yourself.

All of these elements play a part in the things that happen in our society and across the world. The media uses the propaganda to make those who live in that area look like the worst people in the world. Most of the time when the crime is committed in these neighborhoods the person who's involved don't even live there. In any city that you visit they can spot someone like you and know that you're from another town. In these situations you can become a target and be victimized in any hood.

Anyone who comes to Liberty City and visit any part of my hood, I can be your guide. My name carries a lot of weight and I'm relevant in any hood in Liberty City. You can cross the other side of the bridge and get a cup of conch salad, a conch fritter, some soul food, and pick up a drink from the shot house or just take a walk to the corner store down the famous 15th Ave. Your visit can be quite the experience through Liberty City.

Just like the images and the propaganda they display about Africa that it was consumed with sickness and disease, and people starving because they didn't have food to eat, or clean drinking water, and people dying cause they did not have medicine to give them. They provided all of these negative images to keep us away from the Motherland of milk and honey. In reality, Africa is a rich country and is filled with minerals, diamonds, and gold, however, they had a hidden agenda the entire time to reap the benefits and steal from the land. Now, these same situations are happening in Liberty City and different parts of the U.S.A. They are displaying our neighborhood as crime infested and the infrastructure of the buildings are dissipated. I've watched the Liberty City area that I grew up in change from once being filled with African Americans owning the corner stores, the cleaners, the laundromats, and the Mom & Pop businesses, to the cookie lady from the hood who sold chicken and fries or Soul Food from out of her house to make ends meet for her family.

Now other ethnic groups come into our neighborhood selling the same things at their businesses and our people are supporting them and not the Mother who's from that neighborhood. Things have really changed in Liberty City, we can't continue to fall for the banana in the tail pipe mentality. Liberty City has become valuable to corporate America. They have purchased a lot of the properties; from commercial to residential, in order to make a profit and build a community that will drive up the property value and cause the people who have lived there to have to relocate.

The investors will provide a residence that's affordable for a few people but they must qualify by passing a background check and have a qualifying credit score and meet certain income requirements to obtain that housing. This is where the elimination process occurs. Most people in Liberty City have endured some type of hardship along the way due to real life circumstances. These circumstances limit their opportunities in their neighborhood once they build the new condos, and skyscrapers.

Due to some people's financial hardships and lack of transportation, they are limited to purchasing food at the upscale grocery stores that were built in their neighborhood. Oftentimes the local grocery stores cheaper prices for the same items or off brand items are pushed out. This is one of the oldest tactics in the book for the inner-city bait and switch. They switch the housing area from low-income families to single living individuals, or people who work in corporate America. They no longer have to come from the outer parts of the City because they moved closer to their jobs.

The big banks are thinking like tanks on how to maintain and control the uncultivated minds. They want to stay in control of the illusions they presented to the neighborhood by displaying new buildings and saying they're improving the neighborhood by giving them a better quality of life. Every City is a city of dreams but how can the mind consume that vision without it becoming a nightmare. The community must wake up and bring back pride and family values so they can bear witness to the rise of Liberty City and stop sleep walking in someone else's dream about what's best for their community.

Liberty City is a very good place. This community has birthed numerous professional people. Some people have conspired and positioned people in that community. They use their power to plant certain elements within certain communities. The people have to stand up and stop letting their minds get trapped into thinking they have their best interest at heart. Just like we didn't evolve from monkeys, let's stop letting those people make us look like animals in the eyes of the people outside of Liberty City. Liberty City is not new on the map, these areas are well known it can whether any storm.

The area has been rebuilt from many different changes in the environment such as riots, broken homes, poverty, either a mother or father in prison, and losing friends at rapid rates. The community still has the love and support of one another to survive the environment. They have received a lack of support from the school system. They said nothing good came out of Nazareth. Remember, Jesus came out of Nazareth and walked among the people, the thieves, robbers, and the prostitutes. The most powerful figure in our books. He didn't walk on South Beach, or a structure to lure the people.

He was bigger than what the people imagined. Jesus helped people who were lost, in despair, in need of healing, or help with family. When you visit Liberty City, put your mind on the Creator (Jesus) not the people who created the neighborhood or environment. You will enjoy your visit.

LIBERTY CITY

They say it's dangerous in Liberty City but you are welcomed in my hood and you will be respected.

**I don't own a security company or a tour bus that will take you through the city but I hold a leverage to meet and greet and talk to the people in that area. **

1020 The house I grew up in

At Mom and Dad's cemetary
I laid with you when I was a child, I lay with you as a man

The wall on 12th Ave & 63rd Street

15th Ave & 70th Street

The Old Jackson Fish Market

PSU Housing Projects

Pork & Beans Project

Northside Shopping Center

**Miami Northwestern Senior High School
My alma mater**

**Miami Northwestern Sr. High Clinic, named after my
Asst. Principal**

LIBERTY CITY

Liberty Square Housing Project

Holmes Elementary

Holmes Elementary School

Edison Park Pool

LIBERTY CITY

Travis Williams

Scan to pay $WMTBooks

LIBERTY CITY

Here is where I share names out my hood, that are known and unknown without these images. The City wouldn't be molded to the world that a T.V. show gave our town the exposure for many to want to visit. Liberty City is home to these families that helped govern our hood, the Williams, the Warden, the Housers, The Pittsburgh's, The Neworld, The Barkays, The Finales, The Jaxson, The Headhunters, The Bradson, The Turnkey, The Netherlands, The McCrae, and The Jinx.

LIBERTY CITY

These are some of the Nicknames of the people who rep our hood; Rex Cube, New World, HT, Supergray, clean Hat, Cruz, Handy Boo, Red Diesel boys, Addie Debose, grey shoe, Tyrick Green, Norman Cox, Pear head, Frank Roberson, Raymond Robinson, The twins, chill, py, WiWi, Crys, Shoe shine, Handy hoe, Lemondew, Lazi diamond, Alonso Weitz, Day Davis, Prez More, Boogie, Winzel, Cutt, Whineo, big Bills, Jojoes, Duree, Marball, Huddle boy, Papareze, (Rest in Peace) Tanny, ZayHood & Mr. Wonzer, Hoarse, Robbie Scissor, Mcgliide, Hero, Unc Fluze, Dapper Deeds, soursunny, Deke, Dessert ball, haybaby, Squats, hubblegum, Hjockey, Redcap am, Diller, Kertzurt, Daybeat brothers. hoodhound, Zip, Onesie, fig, hoodie Boy, onz, Ho Boy, tickle ground, Pop vus, Lay Boy, j Gutters, Sisser troll, Millersson, Jammer, Hearse, Rizzy Wine, Micah darker, Decks deeds, Refer Read, Coil Black, Little Jal, Torn Katz, Tomo Head, Meow head, Ansin, Kenzie read, Doze hinkle, Jazzy, Alley booze, big Tin, corndog, Joie White, Hog head, Genes, red boy, dark man, cash bingo, Blazer, The sun boys, Tricks, Bose dog, Hearse, clown, zen, Gin, Shell, Mic Low, The Haw, Pak, Whip, France, Blinds, Slack Curve, Key, Fly, Ham, Caine, Tick, Ham, Handy, freewill, Hobbleman, Ladder, Rich Donk, Z Bang, Mailman, Brevard P, Tunk Martini, inky, lk, Leo, Chapel hill, lox, Bose, Donald head, cluck, Gem stone, case Baby, Sam flights,

LIBERTY CITY

(Fighter for the cause) that's forgotten for his stand my hat goes off to the victims of the families that they assume he caused an injury to.

Although they found him guilty he still fights for his innocence. Leg bronze, Ram Brownie, Lazy, Sun Ray, verse, Tz, Nobel hobby, j voss, and Brother, Stickball, Rush, phd, Claw stone, Cloud wine, Hats, Special k, big Tone, Kat Cat, Ike, Fat Lumpkin, Crab, Peabody and his brother Red, Bags, Chec, Zappers, Crew Hall and his Brother Lion Hall. Nail Lane, Donton, 45, Bowkegs, Amoire, Boozend, hunk, hutch, Pothead, Broman, Case, Sheriff, flip, von Jon, Big E, Fat Mic, Fleece, bic, Gangster D, Bombay, Big ron, Icty, Kenny bo, Curt Jones, Pancake, Muscle Head, Na, Puffer, Nailhead, Thirsty, Ulmex, Olive, drunk, Mic Wall, Shug, Hal Robin, Harlem Cone, knight armor, Rice roni, Pearlize, Spencers, Mcglue, hoover rug, Big Snake, Alize, Carve Mags, Eddie red, Time magazine , Pop nail, butter Reese, Scrape, Caps , Jetz, Well Gems, Bratz, Gadgets, doon, Hump, clutch, Ike, hulk, Tab Nat Robinson, Rollins Grocery, Buddy Stevens, Cans, Bern yard, Baby boy, Shake and Bake Tat, Brand Strong, Very, Robbie Heart, The Gram boys, The Bail, Tack, kevrozi, Try one, Zolow , Big Bills, Willow, Stevia, Dueree, Reggie Coery Fowler, Tellis Hall, Corey F, blow leep, hunk, vdub, Ace hack.

About the Author

Travis Williams is the youngest of eight children. He was raised in the middle-class area of Liberty City.

Travis enjoyed his childhood while growing up in Liberty City. He had fun swimming in the summer, skating, riding his bike during the winter breaks and playing with his friends. As he grew older, his life took a different path.

Travis was incarnated for 30 years in a Federal Prison. He was released in February 2020. He is currently rehabilitated mentally and physically and he has a different outlook on life. Travis resides in the Miami area with his wife.

Liberty City is Travis' 2nd book.

Scan to contact me

www.ingramcontent.com/pod-product-compliance
Lightning Source LLC
Chambersburg PA
CBHW050648160426
43194CB00010B/1858